marsh boy
and other poems

Kraftgriots

Also in the series (POETRY)

marsh boy
and other poems

g 'ebinyõ ogbowei

kraftgriots

Published by
Kraft Books Limited
6A Polytechnic Road, Sango, Ibadan
Box 22084, University of Ibadan Post Office
Ibadan, Oyo State, Nigeria
✆ 0803 348 2474, 0805 129 1191
E-mail: kraftbooks@yahoo.com

First published 2013

ISBN: 978-978-918-069-1

= KRAFTGRIOTS =
(A literary imprint of Kraft Books Limited)

First printing, January 2013

dedication

to all my compatriots
forced below deck
forced into torture chambers
for the hyena stomp
with the demons of democracy
then hauled up deck
to sing of chains that shackle the soul
wail for this feast of squabbling scavengers

to all my compatriots
murdered maimed impeached for treason
because they put the province first
because they won't forget their allegiance
to the locked down lowlands

to all my compatriots
made to pay for crimes
for which others are decorated

6 june 2010

acknowledgements

This work wouldn't have been possible without the help and support of the kind and beautiful people around me, whose names can't all be listed here.

Prominent among these are two women, Ms Beatrice Owhonda and Mrs Rose Nwaubani. Except for a poem or two, nearly all the other poems in the second section of this collection owe their existence to these ladies, who acted the Muse. Most of these poems grew out of "good morning" or "good night" text messages to or from these women. Others are comments on particular events or responses to teasers on romance and the family which we tried to figure out. I am sincerely grateful to them.

I am truly grateful to Dr Kontein Trinya, Dr Adeyemi Daramola, Dr Austin Nwabara, Dr Chimdi Maduagwu, Dr (Mrs) Abigail F. Afiesimama, M. H. S. Minima, Glory Worukwo, Stephen Bernard and Ebitimi Nicholas for their sound suggestions, support and friendship.

A special thanks to Prof. G. G. Darah for his counsel and illuminating "Foreword" to this collection.

Mrs Josephine Ogbonna typed and retyped the manuscript, never complaining about the endless changes the poems went through. She deserves my earnest thankfulness.

My family has remained supportive, with Patricia and Taribaralate making their sincere critiques of the unfolding poems. "little christopher is ill" belongs to Nengimote, who is always coming up with intriguing suggestions on subjects and themes to work on. I am indebted to them all.

My profoundest gratitude is to the Father, who has blessed me with a talent that is still developing. Thank You, Father!

preface

This collection, which is the concluding part of a trilogy that includes *the heedless ballot box* and *song of a dying river*, may appear to be one poet's portrayal of a nation redefining and remaking itself; an attempt to shock a complicit community into acknowledging its growing guilt. But no literary work, no work of art, in its entirety, can be said to be the work of an individual, for no writer works in isolation. A messenger, chronicler and entertainer who speaks the mind of his people, his message isn't his, but that of his community. His familiar songs, woven out of everyday events and activities in his society, belong essentially to his society. The idioms, proverbs, particular turns of phrase, inflections and emphases, the images and symbols, which flavour his work and give it a decidedly local colour, rooting it in a particular milieu, belong not to the artist, but to the community out of which the work has grown and derives its full meaning.

In the first section, *marsh boy*, the oppressed minorities of the oil-rich Niger Delta may be the immediate focus, but they're by no means the only figures on this broad canvas of pain, suffering and death occasioned by greed, treachery, repression and an international conspiracy of silence. Modern history is crammed with widespread violations of human rights and crimes against humanity – in Afghanistan, Pakistan and Iraq; in Argentina, Bolivia, Chile, Guatemala and Haiti; in Burma, Cambodia, China and Vietnam; in Chechnya and Tibet; in Indonesia and the Philippines; in the former Soviet Union and Yugoslavia; in Algeria, the Democratic Republic of Congo, Egypt, Sudan and Zimbabwe. In Burma and Indonesia, indigenous peoples are systematically being cleansed off resource-rich lands by brutal regimes, egged on by foreign capital. In Afghanistan, Iraq and Pakistan, thousands are killed every year in a senseless war of civilizations, which pits the crusading Christian coalition forces against suicidal Islamists. In the Middle East, the war for land, which the Zionists and their Western backers make out to be a war for Israel's legitimate existence, takes its toll on the hapless people of Gaza. The wailings from these savaged and threatened communities are heard in every home by the community of the oppressed worldwide, thanks to the internet, satellite television and radio. As the Izon proverb goes, "The eyes of the ram are not sweet as it watches the goat being slaughtered". This section is replete with allusions to some of these tales of horror and heroic struggles from the community of the oppressed and betrayed around the world, demonstrating that poetry, like journalism and medicine, has grown beyond borders to share in the suffering of humanity.

This way, *marsh boy and other poems* goes beyond revealing the injustices meted out to the people of the Niger Delta, or calling for those responsible for these gross violations of human rights to be brought to book, to drawing attention to the humanity of these victims of state-sponsored terrorism and explaining why the marsh boy, an educated cosmopolitan revolutionary denied living room and forced to retreat deeper and deeper into his scarred swamps, doesn't intend to remain the archetypal fugitive forever running from the law. He's learnt from the judicial murder of Ken Saro-Wiwa and his eight compatriots in November 1995, and the roasting of Vicente Menchu and his fellow campaneros in the Spanish embassy in Guatemala in December 1980, that passive resistance often provokes further repression. A modern-day warrior, he draws as much upon stories of everyday life in the Niger Delta as on the history of intrigue, treachery, suffering and resolute resistance to autocracy and savage repression of indigenous people from around the world. Body and soul, a son of his suffering swamps, he stops running and turns to confront the monsters despoiling his rich and once picturesque paradise.

He's determined to bring the fragrance of freedom to slums chained to poverty; to internees of death camps forced to fish in polluted ponds, rivers and creeks and to drink water drawn from poisoned wells and streams.

Forward-looking, *marsh boy* resonates with the anger and anguish of the man in the street, the civil servant, the impoverished farmer and fisherman whose farmland, rivers and creeks have been ruined by oil spillage and seepages from old, poorly maintained pipelines. It echoes the disenchantment of the region's angry, unemployed cynical youth, who are convinced that the road their nation travels leads to "the place of humbling hardship" and "horrific losses". Drawing upon the affective and persuasive power of art, it speaks for the millions being pushed into brigandage by "the clueless clan" running "the larcenous party" and driving "the nation into contemplative poverty". Focused on the internal dynamics of society, it examines the iniquities of our nation within a global context. It probes deep into our base human nature to reveal the psychosocial and economic forces that push us over the precipice and precipitate the disintegration of civilized society.

marsh boy sees a link between oil and gas exploration and exploitation in the Niger Delta, which fails to conform to internationally accepted standards, and buccaneering in the New World in the 16th and 17th centuries. Oil theft and restiveness in the Niger Delta are symptomatic of a decaying and unravelling empire that has long thrived on pillage. Like the Roman Empire in its final years, his nation, which has always seen him as an outsider, looks to his region for a Stilicho to hold the crumbling realm together. Vandals who'd never pass over an opportunity to loot and plunder, the powerful few in the region see this as the opening they need to expand and flourish. "Called to a feast of vultures", they dangle the amnesty carrot before freedom-minded youth, and with mouth-watering bribes persuade many among them to abandon the struggle. Never looking beyond their narrow group interests, these foederati fail to see that their very survival (and, indeed, that of their region) is tied to the success of Stilicho, who must restructure and hold together a fractured federation falling to pieces. Banditti, they fail to see his elevation as their opportunity to transform themselves into leaders of their mistrustful people by bringing to the front burner the issues of true federalism, resource control and the convocation of a Sovereign National Conference to negotiate our corporate existence.

marsh boy appeals to the conscience and sensibility of the reader. Exposing the deep feeling of failure and loss of self-esteem in the region and the contradictions in the structure of our nation, it shows that the politics of oppression and plunder only hastens the disintegration of our fragile federation fast losing the loyalty of vast segments of the polity. It dramatizes the dislocations and pains of a nation where the wanton breach of the Constitution and abuse of human rights encourage marginalized minorities and barbarized communities to engage in redemptive acts of violence while calling for a re-examination of the power relations between the various ethnic nationalities and the birthing of a new and just democratic order that extols our common humanity and instils hope in every grieving heart and struggling, starving home.

The untrained ear reading this poetry of pain and suffering, this poetry of courage and defiance, may hear only the wailing and groaning of a region, which has come to be described as restive, to justify a savage pacification programme put in place to protect a predatory governing elite and a client cabal engaged in plunder and sundry criminal activities in the Niger Delta. The untrained ear may also see the marsh boy not as an aggrieved compatriot whose rights—which include the right to the resources of his region and a healthy, clean, unpolluted environment—have been violated, but as a malcontent, a militant, which is a subtler word for rebel, who must be hunted down and exterminated. Unfortunately, this perception is filliped by the psychopathic kleptocrats who've been in charge of the governments in the various states in the region since 1999. Lacking empathy, narcissistic, manipulative, insatiably greedy, with an exaggerated sense of entitlement and a high proclivity to violence, these parasitic, rapacious rulers and their militias; these vassals of Abuja, whose real loyalty is not to a vanishing empire, but to their deep, leaking pockets, have helped to transform this resource-rich region into a vast killing field and an economic wasteland. There is, therefore, the need to go beyond the surface to feel the trauma of this wounded wasteland.

The tendency has been for some readers to scan through the section that treats public issues and then rush to write reviews that fly in the face of poetic facts. But *marsh boy* isn't just resistance poetry. As the reader would discover, the anger, defiance and cynicism of the first section haven't been carried over into the second. This lighter and seemingly private, ribald component of the collection titled *moonlight blues* continues the quest for true love and harmonious social relationships in a dysfunctional society such as ours. Unlike in the more embracing l*et the honey run and other poems, the heedless ballot box* and *song of a dying river*, which deal not only with the conflict and agony of love, but go beyond romantic love between man and woman to include love for a friend, filial love and love for the community or nation, here the concern is primarily with the ecstasy of love and the sovereignty of passion.

Nevertheless, here as in the earlier collections, love remains a struggle, revealing just how challenging it is to achieve happiness through love. And this is what ties this collection together and, indeed, to the earlier works mentioned above—the struggle to attain happiness through love.

g 'ebinyo ogbowei

11

foreword

This collection, *marsh boy and other poems*, is a welcome contribution to the tradition of poetry devoted to the revolutionary struggles of the people of the oil-rich Niger Delta region of Nigeria. The poems celebrate the radical spirit of the oppressed and exploited people in their relentless quest for equity, equality, and justice. They are songs of anguish, revenge, defiance, love, and patriotism. 'Ebinyo Ogbowei has distinguished himself in this genre of poetic invocation, having published *the heedless ballot box* and *song of a dying river*. The volume is in two sections. The first has 21 poems that explore the tragedy of the region and the tenacious efforts aimed at liberation. The second segment, "moonlight blues", sings of the redemptive power of love and affection. All the poems show dates when they were created.

As a poet-tribune, Ogbowei belongs to a pantheon with ancient and solid roots. The heritage of oral genres of song-poetry is rich with voices that have become universal anthems because they celebrate the triumph of the dispossessed over their predators and exploiters. In the English language literature of the Niger Delta, this tendency hallmarks works of pioneer poets such as Dennis Osadebay, Gabriel Okara, and J.P. Clark. In the 1980s, the literature on the Niger Delta became a handmaiden and companion of the politics of liberation and freedom from terror and exploitation associated with the oil economy. Among the notable poetic voices are Ken Saro-Wiwa, Tanure Ojaide, Odia Ofeimun, Ibiwari Ikiriko, Nnimmo Bassey, Ogaga Ifowodo, Hope Eghagha, Nduka Otiono, Ebi Yeibo, and 'Ebinyo Ogbowei.

The works of these poets have helped to clarify the causes of the militant agitations and armed resistance in the region. Ogbowei's articulation is unique because he is not content with lamentation and denunciation; he salutes and celebrates the heroism of those who recognize the quality of freedom that issues from the barrel of the gun. This heroism is exemplified by the "marsh boy", the dispossessed youth radicalized by the brutal experience in the creeks, swamps and degraded lands of the region. The dedication poem in the first segment pays tribute "to all my compatriots/made to pay for crimes/for which others are decorated." Our "marsh boy" is a freedom fighter and revolutionary intellectual who is in quest of "liberty equality not bread." He is not a mercenary who can be fed with the "poisoned fruits of freedom". The portrait of the "marsh boy" in the title poem shows someone who is a "humble hungry hunter/pushed out of the dining hall/by buccaneering brothers." In response, he becomes the "spear/driven into the soul of the stalker", the bomb "exploding the peace of the pillager", the "marsh boy/quick and handy with a gun."

His poems denounce oppressors and exploiters, especially the local colonialists, the "pillagers blown south by the thirsty winds", the "jackal judges/respectable beneath garments of greed …" The poet is no less unsparing in his attack on Niger Delta opportunists and comprador elements who betray the people's struggle and he refers to them in his "preface" as "parasitic…vassals of Abuja, whose loyalty is not to a vanishing empire, but to their deep, leaking pockets …" for which they have transformed the oil-rich "region into a vast killing field and an economic wasteland."

For Ogbowei, the Niger Delta is not alone; it has its global sisters in all theatres of violence where the voices of resistance and humanism are drowned in blood. Thus, the experiences of the region serve as a microscope for the poet to uncover scenes and memories of terror and their victims. This poetic sojourn takes the reader to places like Spain, Portugal, Bolivia, Chile, Argentina, Guatemala, Cambodia, Burma, the Philippines and other countries notorious for dictatorial regimes. There are also references to events and iconic figures in countries like the

United Kingdom, Russia, China, India, Italy, Greece, Senegal, South Africa, Kenya, Tanzania, Ukraine, United States of America, Sierra Leone and others.

Allusions help the mental compass of readers and Ogbowei's "marsh boy" poems are suffused with them. The references to events, places and personal names broaden the semantic and figurative significance of the verses. But for the average reader the disparate sources and images have a tendency to distract attention from the intellectual and musical pleasure of the poems. The poet has anticipated this difficulty and has provided several pages of glossary at the end of the collection. Another technical matter relates to the graphic representation of place names and persons without the use of capital letters. In the title poem there are several examples like "bosnia", a country in Europe and "somoza", a former dictator in Nicaragua, South America, both recalling the theme of human rights abuse. There are over twenty such references in the poem, "for mamman vatsa", alluding to a Nigerian poet-general killed for an alleged coup plot in 1986. The average reader may recognize political names like "mubarak" of Egypt, "mugabe" of Zimbabwe, and "museveni" of Uganda as African examples of "sit-tight" presidents. The use of these names sometimes produces elegant, phonic sounds, but the unorthodox manner they are represented makes many of them to appear obscure and laboured.

The romantic flourish in the "moonlight blues" section of the volume contrasts sharply with the political and pugnacious idiom of the *marsh boy* poems. The tone of redeeming love and ecstasy is set in the first poem, "now i've found you." After a tortuous pilgrimage with "broken boats paddled by hollow hands", the persona finds the "pink pearl" of the soul and decides not to "go hunting" any more. For the persona, the "half-naked beauty" of "jasmine" is a "seductive fragrance/ that unlocks my box of dreams/is a therapeutic testimony/of an unfolding dawn in the delta." The sight of the woman "eunice" excites similar thoughts: "yielding to the law/written

14

between my ticking thighs/frantic fingers dig into the forbidden pot." The reader will find more pleasant erotic flame in "when he returns" where we have lines such as "knocking silly orgiastic breasts/throwing open pubescent legs/schooled to secure a sealed well/to keep safe its volatile oil." The rhapsodic flow of the verses and marine images in some of the poems blend very well into juicy poetry. The sensuous dialogue and exchange in others soothe the heart and stir memories that many would like to cherish. These thoughts are echoed in the lines, 'with you i'm born again/with you i've a new lease of life/ the dark clouds and storms gone."

Prof. G. G. Darah

contents

marsh boy

Unhappy the land that has no heroes
Unhappier still the land that has need of heroes

Bertolt Brecht

Victory at all costs, victory in spite of all terror,
victory however long and hard the road may be;
for without victory there is no survival.

Winston Churchill

marsh boy

I

locked in the prison of poverty
denied the right to rise
out of holes in sighing swamps
i sing of creeks with crushed dreams
i sing of ponds with decaying hope
i sing of rivers the cargo ships and
      supertankers sail on
i sing of swamps sold to swindlers and
      rustlers
i sing of swamps demanding dignity
      and opportunity
spurned passed over
      i cast aside paddle and net
humble hungry hunter
pushed out of the dining hall
by buccaneering brothers
like locusts have overspread the land
      i sing of ambushed agreements
        that bring us to son my and srebrenica

II

i am the marsh boy
      quick and handy with a gun
i am the marsh tiger
      stalking beneficent tyrants
      swept south by cruel storms
      to secure staked swamps
      stolen in the mean months of '66

i am the evil child who cries too much
                    you say
i am the evil spirit driving the delta round in loops
                    you say

i am the dagger
        driven into the mind of the mugger
i am the assegai
        driven into the soul of the stalker
i am the bomb
        exploding the peace of the pillager
i am the marsh boy
        quick and handy with a gun

III
carpet bomb the bellicose bogs
cauterize clean the cancer
in the sultry south
crimsoning the wounded wetlands

the horse would throw off the rider
mudbugs would be honoured held high
mud hens would roost in palaces

we'd be decked in royal robes
but you dress us in shrouds
we desire liberty equality not bread
but death a liberator
the grave a leveller
you feed us the poisoned fruits of freedom

IV
angry waves pummelling the mutinous marshes
serena securing his loyalty
stilicho shall serve the emperor
strongman from the servile south

22

he'll hold together the torn realm

rumours out of squalid holes
angry waves thresh contentious coasts
and out of friendly places intrigues
out of shadowy hills and baking sands
vengeful cutlasses and foxy axes
hack off the grabbing hands of a dying dominion

angry waves wash away pumpkin kings
snooty hostages triumphant on termite eaten stools
angry waves wash away quislings
promoting prosperity of cruel crowns
have left us outcasts on the fringes of society
vengeful cutlasses cut down the *foederati*
peacocks without plumage without pride

angry waves wash away turkey cocks
commanders wrestling for control of oil
clinging to privileges that deny our humanity
establish the objective merits of war

commanders coveting stone and throne
legionnaires would live forever in the soaring city
recruit us to steal for them the useful objects
recruit us to steal our way to guatanamo
where warriors without judicial guarantee
study the balks to bosnia's peace

V
i am the marsh boy
          quick and handy with a gun
i am the marsh tiger
          stalking beneficent tyrants
romanovs who see in our desolation their prosperity
somozas who see in our destruction their security

infernal crowns a curse to our coasts
would sear on our consciousness
the delta is a death parlour
a place of grief
where we're gathered to hear
the ghouls decide how you deserve to die

tasting the buttery vapour of life in a vodka
i see beyond the caterpillar
chewing leaves buds and flowers
i see the pollinator fluttering in the almond garden

sweeping through eventful graveyards
i see the elusive army of the despoiled
protesting peasants mourning menchu
mourning a bishop bludgeoned outside his garage
denouncing disappearances battered babies
suckling mothers murdered for body organs

suicides without sufficient safeguards
orantes and margarita tied in bed
are charged with a rabid dog
like a raging bear has cracked gerardi's skull

sweeping through eventful graveyards
i see scorched seaside settlements
i see the elusive army of the debased
take the burning brand to the pernicious precinct
a wailing bullet burying a complicit consul
petulant policemen set ablaze a benevolent embassy

i see the sick state crumble like a kicked-in sand castle
a presidential palace strewn across a screaming street
starving criminals scavenging for supplies
dance around the dead and dying
rush into promising stores and warehouses
haul home stereo systems sacks of sugar and flour

VI

how can they live in peace
asks asida sorrowing for her son
dragged into the night
necklaced a mother's joy

how can they live in peace
whose seductive symphony
calls out of ravaged rivers
the avenging demons of destitution

discovering ourselves in a democracy
that lays waste our liberal lowlands
we're lost in a gun-toting kleptocracy

discovering the plasticity of greed
seeing through the bizarre rituals of corruption
we dynamite granite hearts
that see us protesting only as brainless people do

now hear traumatized territories
answer with their quaking and rattling
see sullen rivers carry their cargoes of death
to the sea's exhibit room
where wailing widows wait for sons and spouses
whose footprints the sour sea has washed away

now locked doors are blown open
see palm-greasing patriots
flirting through breached bunkers
to the hall where history is made

now locked doors are blown open
see scheming cowards and cunning criminals
celebrate the valour of partisans
their watchful practised steps
bringing them to thrones others have died for

hear the mimicking bullfinch warn
the monkey who'd be king in heaven
is buried beneath a mountain of greed

hear the hyena howl
the battle for land
is the battle for life
the place of suffering
is a place of learning

25 february 2009

this perpetual paranoia

this game of thrones
that plays out in decapitated capitals
this power play
trading ballots in bleeding streets
this cut-throat politics
that leaves us all diced
that leaves us all cut up
shifting patterns on corleone's chessboard
democracy you say it is

this ideology of terror
that comes with wine women and weeds
this love of the betrayer
this loyalty to the slayer
that bullies us
into taking the name of our abuser
that bullies us
into learning the lingo of the looter
patriotism you say it is

this perpetual paranoia scarring the state
concern for the fatherland you say it is

16 september 2009

27

welcome to our smouldering swamps

welcome to our smouldering swamps
welcome to the swamps of death
our boiling cauldron of loony leaders and dreamers

asawana
wana

you who'd kill your way to oil wells and gas fields
you who'd cultivate our confidence
pounding cross creeks into submission
waltz with us through the starving swamps
waltz with us through the maze of time
come with us to choeung ek
come with us to tuol sleng

asawana
wana

what are schools and clinics to the vanishing ones
what are water pumps and power mowers
what are cruisers and suvs to the swamp dweller
this toothache running needles
through the roof of your head
this bomb ticking in your grasping mind
this running sore draining your sick soul

asawana
wana

what use is rembrandt to the blind
what lesson could he learn from the blinding of samson
what lesson could he learn from a bankrupt painter
preoccupied with costume and form

28

asawana
wana

what use is tchaikovsky to the deaf
what lesson could he learn from the queen of spades
quick-witted crone secure on her throne
knows her signature strengths
won't be tied up in dependent relationships
won't be housewife won't be housemaid

asawana
wana

what use is tchaikovsky to the deaf
can't sprout his dreams in his smouldering swamps
can't play deep-thinking hamlet
trying hard to crack a moral nut
is called upon to play crown and anchor
with acquisitive cousins always must win

asawana
wana

sabra and shatila wailing
a stolen truck wreaks vengeance on blustering braves
smug in an exposed fortress
pleading moans out of heaped tiers of rubble

asawana
wana

a steaming sewage truck explodes across the street
khobar towers totter fall
two errant jets crashing into a crystal hill
the twin towers totter fall

asawana
wana

al taifa takes to sea
a daring dinghy takes on a destroyer
al taifa takes to sea
a bully is bloodied
whines like a wounded dog

asawana
wana

fanatics take the kaaba to kenya
fanatics take the al aqsa south
sow seeds of faith in dar-es salaam
beguile bush
charm a swash to the burial ground of empires

asawana
wana

you who'd kill your way to oil wells and gas fields
you who'd win over wary hearts
pounding contentious creeks into submission
welcome to our sticky swamps
welcome to the swamps of death

asawana
wana

you who think you hold the watches
discover now we've got the time

asawana
wana

26 may 2009

30

hunt down ephialtes

we who've tasted victory
at the marathon with leonidas
we who're obedient to your commands
at the gates of fire make our stand

hurry hunt down ephialtes
betrayer in brick house
says he's the subtle weasel
has rendered the hyena tailless

hurry hunt down ephialtes
hunt down the subtle weasel
would trick us all to our death
to provide his wife an elephant hide

hunt down the shrewd hare
outsmarting lion and hyena
opens the royal chamber
to the intrigues of the harem

would give away gorgo
make her mate of mean amestris
megalomaniac like lady macbeth
opened her ears to the poison of hags

hurry hunt down ephialtes
clever little pig in brick house
turncoat has turned the truculent plains
over to pillagers and sackers

take our deathless message
take the deathless seed
sprouting in schoolrooms and trenches
take it to the master of the tables

able arbitrator touring taverns and docks
networking the blackballed coast
spins this spaghetti of sizzling anger
into sheets of spicy songs

transporting the partisans to tebu
there like themistocles at salamis
beat back the boastful burner
sacking insolent settlements

send him scurrying home
to fight whirling darting firestorms
their fire clouds triggering further fires
exploding valleys and burning plateaux

send him scurrying home
who stole the sacred vessels of the altar
send him scurrying home
who alone can quench the passion
shriveling amestris' mean heart

12 may 2009

the cry of a disappointed doe

this is the cry of a disappointed doe
pining for her philandering buck
this is the cry of a starving city
has kept open the road of life

a wicked wind blows out of the parched north
a thirsty wind blows out of the improvident north
besieged like leningrad
the stubborn city stands her ground
won't give in to genocidal despots
who'd cleanse a race to advance a clan

this is the cry of a city pitilessly pounded
this is the cry of a city starving to death

in the eyes of the agitated
the gory glory of a volcanic rage
tidal waves washing short-changed shores
break the ring of iron around the menaced marshes
shake down wash away arrogant garrisons

the dreams and obsessions of october 1
drain into loot-loosed lowlands
where the dragons of greed
take shifty patriots
pillagers blown south by thirsty winds

this is the cry of a disappointed doe
pining for her philandering buck
this is a smoking gun agreement
a rapist's settlement with a violated virgin

i see them all coming and going
through the revolving doors of my mind
chinasa and chinonso

folake and folarin
halima and hamal
nerissa and neymar
lust ravening dogs beneath their skins
clawing and biting
the growls and howls of hounds
tearing traitorous hearts

this is the success of the he-goat
scrumptious in a stew pot
this is the blood price we pay

a harvest of pain won't cease
a mistake we never stop paying for

3 november 2008

34

for mamman vatsa

the tolling outrage
of a twisted buffoon
breakfasting with war-weary orangemen
the moonflower smile of the spy master
a smile that tickles the confidence of the betrayed

a smile that soothes him to sleep
delivers him to daw suu
meeting with khin nyunt
secure in insein prison

the scheming sword slits the throat
of the favourite of the revolution
the devious dagger hacks down
the golden boy of the revolution

the probing left hand
speaks dark words to jackals
trailing the king of the jungle
tricking him into doing things propitious to them

tricking him into rushing plucked peasants
through steppes of suffering
to a cold place
where dissent and pride
crumble on their knees
worship the lie
that pushes the devotee into purgatory

bring in the man of steel
holds bukharin in the boudoir
where his wife took her life
there prepares his soul
for a dance with the mother of satan

bring in jealous josef
a symphony of nine syringes
at a witches' sabbath
plays up the pain of slashed throats
pleading for reprieve in swelling labour camps

bring in reticent sunglasses in decorated fatigues
bring in the morbid mail clerk from mandalay
battened on the delta
bloodies the irrawaddy
drowns the resistance
bores the nation into submission

bring in the smiling general
mastered at mandala
cleans out sukarno
mops up his red sympathizers

dogs dragging decomposing bodies from stinking streets
reeking corpses clogging rivers and creeks
vultures and crows applaud this patriotism
that degrades a neighbour
that puts pocket above the people

kissinger kissing the komodo
ruttish rifles have ruined chinese skirts
run amok in dili
and at the edges of the archipelago
aceh and new guinea drown in blood

in a ransacked house
a murder goes awry
a joy ride ends in tragedy
hanging from a bridge
two charred bodies
at the bottom of a lake
a telltale plastic bag

in the triangle of death
an ambush goes awry
ruttish rifles rape abeer
can't make souvenirs of mutilated bodies
burn bloodstained beddings
set her home afire

at checkpoints on curvy roads
ruttish rifles bait break granite hearts
take in wailing widows and violated virgins
collateral to cover the debts of the dead

bring in bush blair barak
sling them to the killing tree

ten fingers locked into ten toes
the sentinel reveals
the bearded dragon
in a withering garden
consoling doleful catherine

bring in mubarak mugabe museveni
wasters weighing in with tulio and miguel

bring in biya bashir ben ali
bring in bloodstained bitter-enders
walk them down the *xibalba be*
to the point where history and time meet
walk them down the dark rift
walk them down the cheerless chambers of the heart

bring them to the place of gloom
where dancing skeletons
holding aloft smoking urns
parody the pain and panic of slashed throats
pleading for reprieve in swelling labour camps

29 april 2009

a deranged gun

a deranged gun taxies a trembling jet
through the eye of a hurricane
to a gate that opens into the past

ransom riches have reached rumuekpe
banditry brings beautiful girls and luxury cars

rummy laughter holidaying in montego bay
wakes blackbarts in marine gardens
rustlers roasting oysters for spanish ships

ransom riches have reached rumuekpe
banditry brings beautiful girls and luxury cars

rummy laughter holidaying in montego bay
brings up the charmed *whydah*
laden with loot
drunk on madeira
seeks out sweet maria
breaks her back on a sandbar
spilling her pride and joy
across the floor of a frothy sea

ransom riches have reached rumuekpe
banditry brings beautiful girls and luxury cars

rummy laughter holidaying in montego bay
brings up pirate ships from watery graves
finds fault with loot-minded crowns
that push princes and gofers
outside the fettering freedom of the law
into the sunburst glory of the rocking sea

ransom riches have reached rumuekpe
banditry brings beautiful girls and luxury cars

lightning-swift out of a spooky dawn
cannons explode aboard a drowsy galleon
flickering flames burning ropes and sails
swinging axes flashing cutlasses
blackbeard boards a burning boat

ransom riches have reached rumuekpe
banditry brings beautiful girls and luxury cars

a pirate bash in a hideaway hog
a pistol shot
a swinging sword
a cropped head hangs
from the bow of a sly sloop

ransom riches have ruined rumuekpe
ransom riches bring regal houses and beautiful girls

puerto principe and porto bello taken
panama city is set ablaze
marcaibo mocking the pirate king
cunning longboats fool conceited guns
an enchanting lantern on a treacherous reef
luring weary ships to the chickchamie's nest
the pirate king returns to kingston
morgan returns to montego bay

ransom riches have ruined rumuekpe
ransom riches bring regal houses and beautiful girls

rummy laughter holidaying in montego bay
reveals in the darkness before dawn
a convoy uncoupling from conniving barges
reveals far out at sea
cocaine cash and guns
rendezvousing with risk pooling boats

ransom riches have ruined rumuekpe
ransom riches bring regal houses and beautiful girls

buck raking kleptocrats
protecting oil-dripping pockets
poison the politics of a peckish province
provoke fraternal brutality in wrathful rivers
suck out the soul of the charmed swamps

ransom riches have ruined rumuekpe
ransom riches bring regal houses and beautiful girls

20 april 2009

the tyranny of greed

this is the tyranny of greed
this seductive violence
that snares your scoffing soul
that takes captive your mooning mania
takes it on a tour of killing fields
deep in the despoiled delta

this is the tyranny of greed
this smash-and-grab relationship
that does nothing but grab and hide
that strips us of dignity and humanity
that clobbers kills our crabby joy
scrambling into humming holes

this is the tyranny of greed
like a starving pride
drags down a compassionate seductress
a blockbuster rape on pleading knees
and to kill her shame
pushes squealing rats
into her weeping vagina

2 february 2009

avoid them

out of the mist a voice
wizened witch in a canoe
ebb-tide drifting out to sea

avoid them parasites and politricksters
blown south by thirsty winds
avoid them marauders and murderers
washed on to our welcoming shores

a squall line of thunderstorms
raging rivers of blood
seasons of pain over the pliant plains

avoid them brick house hunters
who see you as prey
avoid them creek haven anglers
who use you as bait
who suck the sugarcane from your farm
then litter your veranda with pulp and peel

mangrove giants sighing in the chilling half-light
night birds touched by treachery has stirred the dead
echo her worrying wail
exploding seaside settlements
bring her back to me
soft belly balming my burning body
milk-full breasts drowning my hungry cries
heartbroken mother fishing out of furious seas
sick souls cast overboard deviant boats

the city by the sea is broken
the city of strife is taken
in her midst groaning and grieving

and did she not always warn
heartbroken mother fishing out of furious seas
sick souls cast overboard deviant boats
did she not always warn
not every han carry cutlass kin kill
yet you get for watch cutlass an han

and did she not always warn
heartbroken mother fishing out of furious seas
sick souls cast overboard deviant boats
did she not always warn
orange yellow fine for eye
how you know 'e sweet

burning fish settlements and yawning graves
bring her back to me
how clear her worrying wail
learn for be sentinel na you hos
cos plenty tem na dere de rascals kin gada

the city by the sea is broken
the city of strife is taken
in her midst groaning and grieving

4 december 2008

the horrors of history

a mocking mob of lunatics and liars
insisting on having the last laugh
whip him up the hill of sorrow
shame him up the tree of fame

their paranoiac psychoses
imperilling the grumpy plains
tyrannized territories caravan their horrors
to him in the hall of justice

broken old bags disoriented derelicts
starving subversives stumbling out of torture chambers
lemon breasts breached to lace banzer's brandy
wail down a thunderstorm

cannons exploding in coastal castles
tomahawks take out wilful warriors
who took philip's bait
sold their city-states to the macedonian menace

raiding ourselves into poverty and inconsequence
how can we now pull out the rusty hooks
lodged in our hurting gills
how can we now league ourselves into relevance
our freedom sealed in his funeral coffer

but out of the deep horizon
dead souls singing to sorrowful swamps
rally the restive region
bring the fragrance of freedom
to internees of concentration camps

and from behind the bars of tarrafal
i hear luandino cry

the day of liberation
is a day of desecration

out of the deep horizon
i hear taras and tambo cry
how dreadfully colourful
the horrors of history

4 july 2010

to brig-gen wuyep

as in a nightmare we find ourselves
in a luckless boat with lots of leaks
making for port
is stranded on a boiling bog
bristling with crocs pythons tigers

frantic screams dying in our throats
we wake up among sahelian siblings
forever squabbling over grub and shelter
are bullied south by smothering sand

we wake up among concerned cousins
cutting out tongues
cutting out hearts
bleed the tribe out of the delta

we wake up among benevolent brothers
playing baccarat in a backroom with a changing bank
station snipers above stormy streets
where we've resolved to make our stand

we wake up among jackal judges
respectable beneath garments of greed
deliver the dying dominion to death squads
who turn our pleasant places into free-fire zones

we're the lowlifes
crawling out of the cracks
of your hissing hearts

mambas we raise our heads
stare you straight in the eye
stare you back your thieving tracks
lightning out of the undergrowth

bullet out of a low branch
we strike before the hunter
can mutter his surprise
bring the battle to his beery body

swimmers snoopers climbers racers
we're the trackers of prowlers
booming through our gushing marsh
destroy its dreamy peace
to balance their blood budget

pit vipers at home on forest floors
as on tree tops
motionless masters of camouflage
silent we wait for loggers and prospectors
booming through our gushing marsh
destroy its dreamy peace
to balance their blood budget

pythons and crocs cool beneath shimmering waters
we're the masters of stealth
waiting for droughty buffaloes and cunning cats
take them down to our watery beds

28 december 2008

we're the killer bees

we're the killer bees
stinging the steaming marshes of your mind
where trampling boots and wolfish fatigues fall
are gathered fuel for fires of freedom
eating up swamp and savanna

greed a thousand plundering saws
exalts itself above assiduous hands
greed a thousand whacking axes
exalts itself above bustling hands

swarms out of dislodged hives
forest floor crawls with fire ants
forest floor crawls with army ants
slapping hands abandon boastful axes
slapping hands run out on self-flattering saws

but smarting feet tearing through bramble and thistle
are dragged down thronged stung to death

in the city of sedition
a skilful sword stands at the parting of ways
a resentful rifle waiting out of sight
sneaks into a well-protected meeting place
in kunkarawa and katsenawa wailing and howling

a flying casket out of the sky
a chorus of crestfallen rifles
loot-lined pockets too long in the limelight
hurrying from the square of fraud
vultures and hyenas quarrel over leftovers

2 october 2008

48

the felon is on the run

the convict is on the run
the jailer too is on the run
for in the place built for punishment
gather weaving twisting swords
schooled to cut out larcenous hearts

the felon is on the run
the enforcer too is on the run
for out of pitiless places pour marabous and bateleurs

the shoplifter is on the run
the shopkeeper too is on the run
for the place built for trade
has become a place of butchery

hawker and retailer are on the run
wholesaler and bulk buyer too are on the run
for the place built for trade
has become a place of execution

the borrower is on the run
the lender too is on the run
for the place built for regulation
has become a place of enchantment

all around parrots and pythons
in a tray with a trimmed lamp
a suicide's skull a suya stick with a scorpion
newt eyes a frog's lap and gizzard of a crow

four perky black goats
tethered to a crocodile staff
planted in front of the market master's office
speak to a barking salamander

calamity out of the cruel city
calamity out of gogorin and gabarin
out of the kingdoms of the north
gather hyenas riding grey horses
they converge on alluring highlands

at twilight trembling phalaris
makes his escape from his burning pile
with him irene
regent to hold on to a crown
plucks out her son's eyes

across town a corpulent metropolitan
crawls out of his burning basilica
a ring around the inferno
a lynch mob launched on a purposive plan
waits to take goat-footed priest
always straying into seductive bedrooms
waits to take a trembling tyrant
to burn him in his bronze bull

3 september 2008

the fumbling king

determined to cleanse the contumacious coasts
determined to drain the defiant wetlands
with flattery bribes and broken covenants
written with the blood of her branded braves
to drain her strength break her resolve

the fumbling king falls
is carried away by the bravissimo of ravenous chauvinists

the provocative hypocrisy of self-serving patriots
teasing the daisies out of his dreams
drives him down a white gravel driveway
winding into the garden of grace
for a neck-snapping kiss with clara harris

the fumbling king falls
is carried away by the bravissimo of ravenous chauvinists

gurgling tides flooding the crabby coast
sandstorms out of the scorched sahel
desolating grief on harassed highlands
scamming sycophants at his table
wheedle him into a shallow grave

the fumbling king falls
is carried away by the bravissimo of ravenous chauvinists

oily words of sharks with shiny teeth
sharper than brutus' dagger
cut until his cunning heart
feels the feral pain of pleading death

the fumbling king falls
is carried away by the bravissimo of ravenous chauvinists

26 april 2009

on the margins of consciousness

I

on the margins of consciousness
grief and anxiety crawl out of melancholic marshes
where the grunts and hisses of feasting vultures
drown the growls of dogs
nimble lively dance themselves into a den of lions

to end the mantra of peace
to incite an apocalypse
a topless dancer
dances her way into a defiant stadium

to yank the heart out of the daring rabble
to kill the swagger in the rebellion
rat eyes peeping out of a burning canvas
seal a deal with crawling dogs

II

what do you seek in sekouba
come watch the september slaughter
come watch camara clobbering conakry
stripping the city of her dignity
come see grace raped to death
come see bah beaten to death

what do you seek in sekouba
come see our brawling barracks
come watch the dadis show
see napoleon riding out to sea

playing snakes and ladders with power players
who'd make the rain fall on their roofs alone
we slide down a dunghill

land by boxes of broken promises
their contents strewn among the sludge
of human waste and mouldy dreams
the morning rain washes into a weary river
reluctant to carry its contraband of death
to coastal communities making each day
with the materials at hand
watching the season
to predict the next fish run
to discover what doors are opening and closing

III

this road paved with good intentions
takes us not to tiananmen gate
this road paved with good intentions
takes us to the gates of hell

this road paved with good intentions
takes us not to the place of dazzling transformations
this road paved with good intentions
takes us not to the place of prosperity and dignity

this road paved with good intentions
carries us to kandahar
this road paved with good intentions
carries us to the city of continual convulsions

takes us to the place of humbling hardship
to the place of horrific losses
where victory is a pillar of smoke
a death sentence executed at night

9 october 2009

the dialectics of corruption

the cruel capital is burning
confusion and keening in kuala lumpur
in kirkuk kabul and karachi
wailing widows won't be consoled
shatter the complacency of profitless princes
celebrating the installation of the rat king

the city of wastrels is burning
in emergency room and arbitration chamber
we study the dialectics of corruption
in schoolroom and courtroom
we study the leaps and glides of kleptocrats
the dazzling dance of bombs and guns
can't keep talib off the poppy trail

marcello moves to new orleans
in the marshes of the mississippi
a conspiracy is cooked
in the marshes of the mississippi
the bruiser borrows a grumpy gun

a wringy rifle rattles a dance hall
a shrill wail shreds the shroud around asarama
her husband hauled home
her wounded women bewailing their virginity
stolen on floors of pharaoh's chariots
risha rebuffs battle-axes
come to console a crushed consort
come to lure her out of her groaning shore

24 july 2009

54

echoes out of dark sepulchral hearts
(to *chief e k clark and prof kimse okoko*)

you called to the feast of vultures
you called to the feast of hyenas
feast on my feverish infants
sloshing through surly swamps

hadizatu mani sold for $500
seeks a beauty beyond her sahelian horror

ten years thunderclouds poured money
ten floods flushed treasuries vacuumed vaults
funneling billions to safe havens
as fetid drains flowed into hungry homes
rodents roaches reptiles
cholera crawling bugs begging bowls
unimpeachable dividends of democracy

hadizatu mani sold for $500
seeks a beauty beyond her sahelian horror

winning over with cognac cash and contracts
wily warriors battling caesar's legion
have made our coasts the elegiac hunting grounds
of a nation most heartily reconciled to death
rumbling bellies fresh from the barricades
take elena from targoviste
marshal marie antoinette to the passionate guillotine

hadizatu mani sold for $500
seeks a beauty beyond her sahelian horror

they that are full of sound and fury
fleeing are taken
perplexed princes pleading for their lives

complicit rifles
concealing slaughterous secrets
kill hollow words of hollow men

hadizatu mani sold for $500
seeks a beauty beyond her sahelian horror

in courtrooms judas judges
chastise larcenous foxes
obsessed with spoil
shrink the mongrel nation
carve it into hereditary chiefdoms
to swell nest eggs
big bank balances in tax havens
prying cameras cannot reach
differ to deng
shy from the fatiguing march to freedom

hadizatu mani sold for $500
seeks a beauty beyond her sahelian horror

an 80th birthday at bibi's bar
the nine lords of darkness
around a cleared table
by a reflecting pool
the cold dying sun
lighting up the wine and stew stains
calculate the blood price
of the economy of plunder

hadizatu mani sold for $500
seeks a beauty beyond her sahelian horror

belching breaking wind
their overbrimming bellies
like the label on a wine bottle
tell their tastes their worth their faith
their crippling cunning their glamorous greed

hadizatu mani sold for $500
seeks a beauty beyond her sahelian horror

hollow words of hollow men
echoes out of dark sepulchral hearts
thunderstorms over the spumous south
kindle fires in the retreating sahel

hadizatu mani sold for $500
seeks a beauty beyond her sahelian horror

a howling horror in piata libertatii
from sanaa to salamiyah
a dreadful victory
a howling horror in munificent marshes
from numan to new bussa
a wailing nightmare

hadizatu mani sold for $500
seeks a beauty beyond her sahelian horror

26 july 2009

57

how many mays more

many mays have passed
many rainy seasons have come and gone
but the turning seasons
haven't turned our fortunes
haven't refreshed famished farms
haven't dulled the plaguing pains
we pray long hours
in longsuffering churches
these rain gods
withholding rain from thirsty holdings
should caringly remove

many mays have passed
many rituals performed
many sacrifices offered
still the drought endures
ravenous fires continue
to eat up the starving land

communities can't coalesce into a nation
tribes can't be welded into a state
wonder how many mays more
how many sacrifices more
before famished farms are refreshed
before the curse on the clan is broken
before locusts eating down
the greens are cleaned out

29 may 2009

this larcenous party

this party plunging the nation
into contemplative poverty
this larcenous party
always straying from the law
    is a black
      h
      o
      l
      e
    gobbling
      up
     everything
        that
            swirls
                around
              a quasar
         drawing
    in
        adventurers
            cutthroats
            con men

            the constrictive chaos
            at the heart of the party
        crushes
    kills
the nation's potentials
    draws her
      down
        draws her
        into
        a

                    death
          s
                p
                    i
                r
          a
        l
        a crucible of corruption
          crony capitalism
      duplicity
   squirming poverty
paranoia
      exploding
          gang violence
          a putrid
                justice system

a people praying for change
a people purposed to determine their destiny
look through a violent window
to see a parade of perfidy

                sitting atop the leaning tower of greed
                are the drunken dogs
                running the pernicious party

the pendulum of change swings
but each cycle throws up
the same clueless clan
whose incontinent greed
pushes a once prosperous province
                    over
                the precipice
                into
                    a

black
h
o
l
e

24 june 2010

shifting fault lines

(to ratko mladic and sarkin bello)

studying these shifting fault lines
the brew of conflicting loyalties
churning the soul of the nation
i stumble on the bludgeoned body of baby charles
dumped on the doorsteps of our distraught home
the word Ա/ dr with a fork
carved on his bloated belly

i stumble upon those restless ghosts from mass graves
stalking xenophobic rifles
cleansing chary churches

i hear the spine-tingling screams from sniper alley
trailing loot-laden slayers
slogging through rising rivers of blood

to defeat the gloating envy and deceit
locking down the fractious floodplains
locking down the plucky plateau
to defeat the backstabbing greed
corrupting farmer and fisherman
hunter and oyster gatherer
to defeat the overreaching greed
draining the liberal lowlands
i see them pluck out the green white green
the plunderer's flag of pride
hoisted on the conscience of the free

25 february 2010

amnesty

I

am i marx
sacrificed on the altar of profit
is forced to father an illusion

am i mary
singing to stir the conscience
        of our strange assembly
to hammer the granite hearts
        of a brutal band
singing to alert ravished rivers
        this land is your land

no i'm sosa
with no sleek mercedes to ride in
poor exile with no place to sing
poor exile sighing for spoofed slums
with their pongy memories of poverty and pain

II

can i like cooke
soul stirrer stirring the chain gang
sing of peace in the valley
when a green gun
out of a seamy hacienda
has her hand in my pocket
twists our wonderful world away

can i like carly
drum the defining pains of the bogs
good friday
give my life to my wife
with carter will small-axe me

rat-race me to tosh and braithwaite

can i like claude
sing of the sins and secrets of lynching streets
sing free the wild goat
with its chains of gold
dragged into the knacker's yard
hopelessly upward looks at the sacrificial smoke
pluck out the punitive pole
to which it is tethered

can i like teddy
the whole town laughing at me
shout and scream
come spend the night with me
come learn love's lifting lingo

III

the tide is out
exposing her mooning mud
on which are etched
the crimes and shame of the swamps

plodding through the humming mud
we dredge up mortifying memories
silt-laden floods would bury
the coins with which we were bought
the casks of wine in which we drowned
the swords and guns with which we laid low the
                                    conniving coast
balls and chains with which we dragged off complicit
                                    communities
delivered them to smart slavers
won't take on the vengeful anopheles
stayed off our buzzing waterways

today other traders out of the retreating sahel
ravenous drovers driven south by the advancing sahara
rustlers charmed south by the christmas tree
and we take them in who trade in death
vacate our beds for
give our daughters to
blood-dripping swords winning us over
with spoils from self-sabotaging swamps

IV

can i like bach
perform for you the passion oratorio
perform for you the empire of passion
where independence ends in hell
a bleeding dream cut in two
by the train of death

can i like brahms
play a requiem for ruined rivers
perform romantic variations of the song of destiny
for friends sacrificed to save a sick state

can i like cox
make you see the pink panther
prompting purposeful peronistas into the plaza de mayo
pushing mothers of harvested babies off death flights

can i like cox
compel campaigning abuelas
to carol carter and congress
draw down to goose green
draw down the iron lady
to do down dapper dictators
bring them in the caravan of death
to read the book of revelation before grasset

can i like rizal
paint for you the double-faced goliath
pushing you to the stake
to which your father is tied
paint for you the hands
reaping your sons out of segunda's womb
scattering your dreams in the desert of greed
paint for you the malevolent mob
washing in your blood its impurities
paint for you the jazzy nightmare of the red rage

can i like bernardo
committed to cutting off the royalists at linares
mobilise a militia
ride through a tightening ring of fire
to teach the lads
how to live with honour
how to die with glory

can i like mehta
make you see in cloud-draped sun sinking into the sea
the warrior mother slaying the dragon king

no i'm sosa
with no sleek mercedes to ride in
poor exile sighing for spoofed swamps
with their pongy memories of poverty and pain

16 october 2009

moonlight blues

A bliss in proof and prov'd, a very woe;
Before, a joy propos'd; behind a dream.
All this the world well knows; yet none knows well
To shun the heaven that leads men to this hell.

William Shakespeare

we are for each other; then
laugh, leaning back in my arms
for life's not a paragraph

And death i think is no parenthesis

e e cummings

now i've found you

now i've found you
        my pink pearl
why should i go on hunting
now i've found you
        pearl that's my soul
why should i go on hunting
the day's done
the weary sun's gone to bed
and out of the hostile horizon
arrogant oil boats
dragon boats spitting fire

conned canoes paddled by grabbing hands
crawl out of scarred creeks
broken boats paddled by hollow hands
crawl out of burning creeks

souls of the departed
can't find a place of peace
can't find a place of protection
souls of the neglected
homeless hungry disrobed of dignity
souls sold huddled in slave ships
return to trouble the treacherous creeks

now i've found you
        my pink pearl
why should i go on hunting
why should i risk a blackout
tempt these tired lungs
tempt the tide and sharks

the dead don't dance
        my pink pearl
the stone's hard
the stone's hard
apply fire to it
and soon it cracks

so now i've found you
        pearl that's my soul
why should i go on hunting

17 october 2009

jasmine

this teasing dragon
that locks my joy
in provocative hips
swaying so seductively
to feisty flutes marimba and djembes
this humbling half-naked beauty
her signature steps
whispering of weaning ecstasies
that break the bars
of cramping experience and precepts

this seductive fragrance
that unlocks my box of dreams
is a therapeutic testimony
of an unfolding dawn in the delta

14 february 2011

71

eunice

with you eunice
i am like the little boy
left alone in the kitchen
looking longingly at the cookie jar
he swore he won't touch

yielding to the law
written between my ticking thighs
frantic fingers dig into the forbidden pot

dripping honeysuckle nectar
bugles twining hunger
playing in reticent groins

blows away the agreement
has screened out hummingbirds and butterflies
has hedged out the horny goat
won't be kept from a fragrant feast

8 march 2010

72

this closed frontier

these walls
built to keep us apart
this closed frontier
keeping us permanently separated

what tunnel runs under the city of sin
what gallery runs under this garden
of churning resentment and fear
would bring us away from the death strip
to the soul's healing home
where the shatterproof walls
in our hearts and heads are taken down

23 september 2009

why can't we go now

why can't we go now
you and i
alone at the seashore
the creeping darkness throwing her veil about us
the stars peeping out of cloud curtains
hurrying out to sea
to where growling thunder
announces the meeting's agenda
wink their approval

why can't we go now
rocking on waves washing our wounded shore
the ferry is waiting
the dolphins are calling
summoning us to belysa's billet
far out at sea
where the weary sun sizzled down to bed

though you say nothing
i hear your hesitant heart beating out your approval
i see the fire in your yearning eyes
the dancing flames from your yielding groin
the hunger of a starving seal
drawing her out to fishing grounds
far out at sea

so let's leave now
for belysa's billet
alone on her lulling lounge
explore the locked rooms of your hesitant heart
make a map of your moaning body

9 june 2010

74

waking up without you

waking up without the warmth
of your sumptuous body
smothering the fire
burning in my groin

without your smiling embrace
smothering my febrile heart
listening to its blues
trying to understand its jive

without your kiss that whispers in the mouth
silencing the minister's screaming argument
the deep-focus doubts
whose tremors ripple through my body

without your burrowing tongue
a deflated balloon threading its way into the heart
penetrating well-protected silos and tunnels
to neutralize nukes and batteries
targeted at foes we're shocked
to find are family and friends

leave me dream keeper
traveller without luggage
shivering alone in a leaky canoe
fast drifting out to sea

26 august 2008

woe is the man

woe is the man
whose heart is a cold stony cell
not a fragrant garden
where resourceful songbirds
reveal the wisps of themes
that link the lover's disparate movements

woe is the man
whose room doesn't keep hold of
the rousing aroma of her snaring smell
whose room isn't lit
by her stirring smile

the flower in the tray
the steaming coffee to start your day
your longing hand hasn't forgotten
the dessert not served at your candle lit dinner
plucks nibbles her muskmelon breasts

28 january 2009

prisoner of my past

prisoner of my past
prisoner of my fears and hatred
i carry on my back the clan's guilt
a corpse crawling with maggots
the stink beating back finger-pointing friends
have accused fresh-face akugo of witchcraft
battered bleeding is left to die in a shack

i am famed handel
before fickle audiences
downcast thinks of quitting
deep in debt plays his farewell concert
but april showers wash away the debtor's prison
blow open the floodgates of inspiration

i am dark-haired beethoven
sad slave at the keyboard
enduring taunts from name-calling neighbours
ravening dogs out of the shadows of sabotaged dreams
is clawed fanged out of the door of the heart
denied dribbled to stardom
sits smiling with wilhelm
through the holy song of thanks

13 june 2009

demons of our wounded past

this lonesome night bats and owls
are loath to leave their lairs
the somnolent drone of rain on roof
the wind a howling hound
pushing hard opens the barred door of the heart
ushers in the vengeful ghosts of our murdered marriage

i fall off to sleep
hearing those beguiling voices
that wheedled your lewd heart
charmed it off its high stool
charmed it to the smooching dance floor

i fall off to sleep
hearing the teasing whispers of dissembling wives
coaxing a mousy nanny goat
to the smothered mate watering hole

breaking through the shimmering veil
four familiar faces you hang out with
haggle off your mask of modesty
haggle off your clock tower cloak
leering eyes on moaning breasts
feverish fingers dig deep to unlock
the wet gates between your widening thighs

like a haunting song
that keeps playing in the ear
long after the band has stopped
and the applause of the thrilled crowd has died
feverish fingers go on digging
calling out of the howling depths
the damning demons of our wounded past

12 october 2008

the bridewells of the heart

I

what can i say to you sybil
what arguments can i advance
to silence the screams from an abused childhood
what incantations can quiet
the dissonant voices from a violated past

shrieking ghosts from the petulant past
siren me to the bottom of the column
where hot hearts
calculate the grumbling cost of grudge

II

following the run of our marathon purposes
we've walked self-centred streets
that end in the swamps of shame
we've travelled troubled roads
that carried us through the sullen desert of the mind

III

these are the whispering eyes
    peeping from behind purple rose curtains
    keep calling us back to tiki's room

these are the enchanting voices
    calling from behind barred doors
    dance us down haunted hallways

these are the lulling lips
    that rope and drag us prisoners
    down whispering holes

to the bridewells of the heart
where we play dungeons and dragons
with brigands who argue
la meilleure facon d atteindre votre
ton but c est par le fusil

6 june 2012

wounding words

gusting gales of gossip
surging storms of slander
contrary currents of public opinion
the bridge of faith shudders founders

wounding words draw no blood
wounding words leave no scars
wounding words bury their barbs
deep in the soul where no scan
or surgeon can find them

but the seasoning sorrows
and teaching pains produce pearls
covetous tongues can't help but praise

yes the pealing pains
pushing us from passions that kill
make us perfect in HIM

28 april 2010

when he returns

when he returns rosanna
when he returns
he'll separate bleating goats
their erotic meters always running
from zippy leaping rutting rams
short season head-banging butting for ewes
baa baa soon stray from the flock

charm from the lake rosanna
charm from the lake the rake
trapped in the spotlight
beguile bring home the jabber
smart strong rangy
fights his bouts in bed
knocking silly orgiastic breasts
throwing open pubescent legs
schooled to secure a sealed well
keep safe its volatile oil

beguile bring home the he-goat
doesn't have enough meat
for a factory farm kill
barbecues on the garden grill

21 september 2008

moonlight blues

moonlight blues heavy stormy
out of the orchestral chambers
of a lively lecher's heart

how crushingly dull life would be
if there weren't well-oiled holes
men dream and scheme to crawl into
plead and pray to be helped out from

how mournfully dark the world would be
if there weren't charming holes
sniffing he-goats work so hard to fall into

24 october 2007

with you

with you i'm born again
with you i've a new lease of life
the dark clouds and storms gone
the chilly wind out of the churning sea
bundles us on a bench on the beach

with you i'm young again
the joys rising tides of hope return
flood my heavy heart
clean out the disappointments and anxieties
clogging coronary arteries

with you i return to our secret garden
where colourful butterflies and courting songbirds
expressive among blue-eyed daisies
and wood anemones in bloom
mocked our juvenile reticence
urged us seal the easter miracle with a kiss

oh the fire it kindled
it's been burning ever since
driving me deeper and deeper into the charming hole
from which no man crawls out
with his head high in the sky

but the humbling hole is a pleasant place
the humbling hole is a honey pot
the humbling hole is a place of beginnings

8 april 2011

the rhythms of love

I

can i help but kneel before you
    help but crawl in
can i help returning to you
    even as the bucket
repeatedly returns to the well
anxious yet calmly descends
hits its liquid assets
bowing bubbling is drawn down
a rocking pleasure
a knock out joy
heavy weary is hauled up
to return repeatedly
to the humbling hole

can i help but stand naked before you
    help but crawl in
to find faith and comfort
in a lightless hole

II

to fall before you
to crawl up to you
and to find you
reaching up to pull me in
to help my fumbling hand
unlock the wet gates
to help me through a panting path
that winds up the heart's healing home
isn't that pure heaven

22 october 2010

red hot lips

scarlet lips
schizoid lips
what do they say to me
do they speak of passion and pain
would they open to speak
of sorrows scouring the soul

red hot lips
are barred gates
locking dragon secrets
we're burning to learn

27 august 2009

the harmattan is here

the harmattan is here
cracked lips
split soles pleading to be hidden
in snug leather shoes

in bed sandpaper soles scratch
tear tender calves and shins

but can these shred the nodding lizard
delirious shaft plumping deep
finds oyster joy
at the bottom of a wind-whipped bay

23 january 2009

the dream of every lass

to fall in love
to be in your lover's arms
to look into his eyes
and to see a light
not a consuming fire
to listen to his heart
and to hear the whispering
flutter of a butterfly
hovering over a rose apple
not the clattering hooves of a he-goat
running from bitter breasts
despoiled despised
would embroider a telling tapestry
lure a lecher to a watering hole
serve him his son's brains and penis
steaming *nkwobi* stings to life
the coiled cobra between his legs

to fall in love
to be in your lover's arms
to look into his eyes
and to see a luminous path
winding up the mountain
to the stars
the keys to the doors of heaven
jingling at the end of a silver chain
secure on your wrist

this is the dream of every lass
this is the dying dream of the tearful teenager
with a sweet singing voice
obese abused laments her lot

turbulent teasers in a brandy balloon
choreographing the raptures and regrets of a fling

20 august 2008

when i fall before you

when i fall before you
when i kneel to kiss you
to pledge my heart to you
isn't it because you're a goddess
we all crawl to worship

or is it because the dance is on the sighing summits
those heaving hills drawing down the lusty climber
to their milk run joy
because the dance is in the ravine
between your twining legs

or is it because the dance is in my loins
because i see a fallow farm
pleading for the planter's return

when i fall before you
when i crawl before you
is it because i see a door i must plough through
the door i was pushed through
nameless voiceless into an anxious room

but today the anxious voices
silenced screened out
their dreams and fears rouletted
reveal not the room's cloggy bed
but chess masters in a divan
refining the soul of the game

the door opens to the sea
a defiant dinghy daring a destroyer
stalker and prowler studying kalbani's dream
a kiss on the nose
washing away the vomit from the sea

the door opens into a graveyard
where we talk with the ungrateful dead
where we listen to the anthem of the sun
watch the bee dance of contented courtesans
pointing us to fleshpots
deep in the lemon grove beyond

10 april 2009

a rare garden

what feeling words
so colourfully can paint
the ache in my groin

what flaming words
so luminously can express
the hunger all night
weaving its ornate pattern
in my horny heart

i will always love you
siren-sweet whitneyed into my ear
triggers a quake
a tsunami that sucks us
far out to sea
deposits us in the mermaid's fun room

even now
the signature your panting nails
scratched on my back
surfboard riding wanton waves
yearns for your swabbing kiss

even now
as the scent of begonias in bloom a bee
your plump perfumed body
pulls me into you

and as i drill deeper
hitting the yielding aquifer
as i drink the sweetness
of your mango breasts
i realize just what a rare garden you are

6 march 2009

my pudding butterfly

i've looked into eyes lit with hope
i've looked into eyes dark with despair
i've looked into stony eyes vowed to silence
the fires of hell burning in their depths

but when i dance with you
i see the sun in your eyes
i hear a tripling trumpet tapping out elmer's tune
flitting fingers tracing this fluttering heart
a nectar-drinking tiger swallow-tail
dipping vibrating hovering over garden plants

the chatty charango bridging moods
jazz drums pacing this throbbing heart
a swinging sexy sax announces
i've got a girl in mgbodo

the liquid piano
with rowing chanters
brings me to the bank of the choba river
brings me to beatrice
my pudding butterfly

25 july 2008

a libretto i hear

when the curtains of heaven
are pulled across the sky
hiding hyel-taku's face from earth
and mulungu repeatedly releases cannons
their trajectories searing ribbons of light
shredding the darkness over the crippled land
and rushing winds whipping up
dust dead leaves twigs poly bags
disfiguring the destitute district
send us scurrying from howling streets

it's not thundering anger on sinai i hear
it's a libretto i hear
i hear him proclaim
a beaming beauty i bequeath
beside beatrice a throne a crown

fingers flying over the keyboard
a makossa rhythm swells surges
seizes charango and rhythm guitar
clarinet and cornet punch in
talking drums and swaying tambourines
wiggling marimba and maracas
dance us out of sick streets
into the heart of time

10 november 2008

this pleasant habit
(in the background Gregory Isaac's *Night Nurse*)

aren't you the strongest wine
i've ever drunk

a quaff from this overpowering bottle
leaves me bombed
     crushed
      chained
dished addict
  i find myself
   always
   reaching for the volatile bottle

who's it
would help break
this agreeable habit
that leaves me slave
of the queen of spades

19 october 2009

my rooster won't return to roost
(for bola ige)

I

my rooster crows to wake me up
my rooster crows to remind me
of duties begging to be completed

my cackling cock warns me
of the cat-footed intruder
of sneaking danger
lurking in the shadows
crawling across the courtyard

it's eerily quiet here
what disaster
what pestilence
what marauders
have invaded my homestead
what hackers
have hacked down my life tree

it's eerily quiet here
yester eve my rooster didn't return to roost
my rooster didn't crow to close the day

II

vicious ivan
fearful of the tatars
sticks to the cossack trail
thirsty ivan
would drink from the volga
takes kazan
takes out the turkic threat

96

backstabbing bandit princes
their canes now slashing swords
defend not the river's trade
defend not the city's fort
slash each other's throat

it's eerily quiet here
my rooster won't return to roost
my rooster won't announce another dawn

III

a bullet brings down mboya
a monstrous plot brilliantly conceived
a monstrous plot brilliantly executed
carves up a querulous republic
and out of widening cracks
crawl the masquerades of our malevolent past

mukeka knows too much
kariuku talks too much
hauled up ngong hills
should pacify the starving pride

four familiar rifles sneak into cicero's closet
four regular rifles wrestle down a renegade
two perfect murders brilliantly executed
wailing in the waltzing west
a collusive congress is crushed
is buried in a landslide

it's eerily quiet here
my rooster won't return to roost
my rooster won't announce another dawn

28 november 2008

little christopher is ill

little christopher is ill

his head is pounding
his teeth are rattling
his body is quaking

christopher has a fever
christopher has malaria

i'm cold i'm cold
i'm cold he cries

little christopher is weak
his throat is bitter
his joints are aching
his breathing is laboured
our bubbly boy can barely stand

little christopher is weak
his appetite has gone on a long journey
it doesn't plan to return soon

the doors and windows are screened
but the breezy boys
gusting in and out
always leave the lobby door open
inviting the mosquitoes to a feast

the mosquitoes are filled
but little christopher is ill

19 may 2010

glossary

abuelas (Spanish): lit. grandmothers; Associacion Abuelas de Plaza de Mayo (Association of Grandmothers of the Plaza de Mayo, but more appropriately, Association of Grandmothers of Children Who Disappeared or Who Were Born in Captivity); an association of mothers of the victims of Argentina's Dirty War (1976 – 1983) established to find out what happened to their children who were kidnapped, tortured and killed and their grandchildren (babies kidnapped with their parents or born in captivity).
Formed in 1977, the abuelas also wanted restitution for "the missing ones" (*los desaparecidos*), to trace the children kidnapped during the country's military dictatorships, restore these children to their legitimate families, prosecute those responsible for their disappearance and to prevent similar human rights violations from occurring in the future.

akugo (Igbo): a feminine name; lit. wealth of the eagle; genuine wealth (as opposed to ill-gotten wealth).

amestris (Persian): lit. friend; wife of the Persian king Xerxes I (480 – 465 BC) and mother of Arterxerxes I (465 – 424 BC), reputed to have been a jealous woman and a cruel despot who engaged in human sacrifice.

asawana (Ijaw): an Ijaw battle cry; a salutation used by Ijaw warriors to which the response is *Wana!* Today the word has acquired other meanings. For example, "You wan make I *asawana* you? (You want me to kill/execute you?)
An onomatopoeic expression, *asawana* conveys the ability of young Ijaw warriors to appear and disappear in a flash. The noun *wana* (or the adjective *wana wana*) means a flash or sudden appearance and disappearance, so that one doubts if what one has seen is real. It could also be used to describe

an illusion.

banzer: Gen. Hugo Banzer Suarez (10 July 1926 – 5 May 2002); soldier and politician, who was president of Bolivia from 1971 – 1978 and 1997 – 2002. One of Bolivia's most repressive leaders, Banzer was intolerant of dissent and freedom of speech. He employed whatever means that was available to him to stifle dissent, establish law and order and to assert his authority. And these included press censorship, using troops against striking mine workers, invading and calling on the Air Force to strafe protesting students of San Andres University in La Paz.

bernardo: Bernardo O'Higgins (20 August 1778 – 24 October 1842); leading national hero of Chile and one of its founding fathers.

bukharin: Nikolai Ivanovich Bukharin (9 October 1888 – 15 March 1938); a Marxist theoretician, Bolshevik revolutionary, Soviet politician, economist and journalist; one of the most prominent victims of Stalin's Great Purge (campaign of political repression and persecution of dissidents and groups perceived to be acting against the Soviet state and the Communist Party) in the 1930s.

camara: Capt. Moussa Dadis Camara, a former officer of the Guinean Army, who served as the President of the National Council for Democracy and Development (CNDD), which seized power in a military coup d'état on 23 December 2008 after the death of President Lansana Conte, a dictator who had ruled the country for 25 years.
Shot in the head in an apparent assassination attempt on 3 December 2009, he now lives in exile in Ougadougou, capital of Burkina Faso.
Soldiers loyal to him have been blamed for the massacre of 157 civilians and other atrocities that took place on 28 September 2009. On that day, opposition members had gone

to the Stade du 28 Septembre in Conakry, calling on Camara to step down. That peaceful demonstration was met with brute force. The demonstrators were fired on, knifed, bayoneted and the women gang-raped, resulting in 157 fatalities and over 1,200 injured.

carly: Carlton Barrett (17 December 1950 – 17 April 1987); the king of one drop rhythm, a percussive drumming style, and an important member of Bob Marley and the Wailers.

chinasa (Igbo): a personal name; lit. the Lord answers.

chinonso (Igbo): a personal name; lit. the Lord is near.

choeung ek: the best known of the sites known as **The Killing Fields** of Cambodia, where the Khmer Rouge executed about 17,000 people between 1975 and 1979.

cicero: James Ajibola Idowu Ige, better known as Bola Ige (13 September 1930 – 23 December 2003); Nigerian lawyer and politician, who was Second Republic Governor of old Oyo State(1979 – 1983) and served as Minister of Mines and Power (1999 – 2000) and Minister of Justice (2000 – 2001) in the government of President Olusegun Obasanjo. Also known as the Cicero of Esa-Oke, he was shot dead in his bedroom in his home in Ibadan on the night of 23 December 2001 while his police guards were away from their duty posts. They all had gone for dinner!

clara harris: a Houston, Texas woman convicted for killing her husband, Dr David Harris, by running over him three times with her Mercedes S430 in a parking lot after finding him with his mistress, Gail Bridges. She now serves a 20-year sentence for this crime.

claude: Claude McKay (15 September 1890 – 22 May 1948); Jamaican-American poet, novelist, journalist and essayist, who dedicated his life to writing verse that promoted spiritual and humanitarian social and political values; a major literary figure of the Harlem Renaissance.

cooke: Sam Cooke (22 January 1931 – 11 December 1960); an American gospel, R & B, soul and pop singer, considered to be the inventor of soul music. A songwriter and an entrepreneur, Cooke participated in the American civil rights movement.

Allusions are made to "Chain Gang" and "Wonderful World", which are among some of his most popular songs.

cox: Robert Cox; crusading British journalist who as a writer of the English-language *Buenos Aires Herald* between 1976 and 1979, when he was forced to flee Argentina, used the Herald to publicize the cases of some of the 30,000 *los desaparecidos* (the disappeared/the missing ones), thereby saving their lives. The desperate mothers of these victims turned to Cox and the Herald, because Argentine publishers and journalists, fearful of military reprisals, elected to remain silent.

daw suu: lit. Aunt Suu; Aung San Suu Kyi (19 June 1945 –); winner of the Noble Peace Prize in 1991 and other international prizes; member of Burma's lower house of parliament and leader of the National League for Democracy, a non-violent political movement that won the general elections in Burma in 1990, but was denied the opportunity to govern the country as the results of the elections were nullified by the Gen. Than Shwe-led military junta.

Active in politics since 1988, she spent fifteen of the last twenty-one years under house arrests and bans.

deng: Deng Xiaoping (22 August 1904 – 19 February 1997); Chinese politician, statesman, theorist and diplomat; paramount ruler of the People's Republic of China from 1977 until his death in 1997.

Although lower-ranking leaders of the Communist Party

are blamed for ordering troops from the 27th and 28th Armies of the People's Liberation Army to clear the Tiananmen Square of the 10,000 protesters gathered in the Monument of the People's Heroes in 1989, Deng is believed to have given the crucial order to shoot and kill.

elena: Elena Ceausescu (7 January 1916 – 25 December 1989); wife of Romania's Communist leader, Nicolai Ceausescu, and Deputy Prime Minister of Romania, who was executed with her husband after a show trial by a military tribunal that found them guilty of genocide, damage to the national economy and abuse of power.

ephialtes (Greek): lit. nightmare; traitor who, hoping for a rich reward from the Persian king, Xerxes I, showed the invading Persian forces a route around the mountain pass of Thermophylae, where Leonidas and the allied Greek forces were resisting the invaders. This treachery helped the Persians win the Battle of Thermophylae in 480 BC.

foederati, sing. **foederatus** (Latin): tribes living on the fringes of the Roman Empire, who were neither Roman colonies nor granted Roman citizenship, but were bounded by treaty (foedus) to provide contingents of fighting men to assist Rome in time of war; allied states; mercenaries.

folake (Yoruba): a personal name; familiar and diminutive form of the feminine name **Oluwafolakemi**; lit. the Lord has made me rich.

folarin (Yoruba): personal name; familiar and diminutive form of **Adefolarin** or **Olufolarin**; lit. born into affluence/royalty.

gerardi: Juan Jose Gerardi Condera (27 December 1922 – 26 April 1998); Guatemalan Roman Catholic Bishop and human rights defender bludgeoned to death in the garage of his home in Guatemala City.

gorgo: daughter and heir of Cleomenes I, king of Sparta (520 – 490 BC) and wife of Leonidas, king of Sparta.

hadizatu mani: a citizen of Niger Republic and victim of slavery. Under the customary practice of Wahiya, Hadizatu was sold into slavery at the age of twelve. Her master, Alhaji Saulaymane Naron, sexually assaulted and subjected her to psychological and physical abuse for nearly ten years. Hadizatu took her case to the Community Court of Justice of the Economic Community of West African States (ECOWAS), which ruled in her favour.

hyel-taku: the Supreme Being among the Bura-Pabir people of Taraba State in Northern Nigeria.

insein prison: a notorious military-run top-security prison near Rangoon, the old Burmese capital, under the control of the State Peace and Development Council. Used mainly for holding political dissidents, it once had Nobel Peace Prize winner and leading face of the pro-democracy movement, Aung San Suu Kyi, as an inmate.

khin nyunt: Lt. Gen. Khin Nyunt (11 October 1939 –); soldier and politician who was Chief of Military Intelligence and Prime Minister of Burma (25 August 2003 – 10 October 2004).
Following a power struggle within the ruling junta, Khin Nyunt was removed from the premiership and later arrested and tried by a Special Tribunal inside Insein Prison on allegations of corruption. Found guilty, he was handed a 44-year suspended jail sentence.

**la meilleure facon d atteindre votre
ton but c est par la force le fusil**
(the best way to achieve your goal is by the gun)

learn for be sentinel na you hos
'cos plenty tem na dere de rascals kin gada
(learn to be a sentinel/watchman in/over your own house
because many a time the rascals gather there)
A Creole proverb that admonishes extra vigilance over one's
household, especially the need to carefully select and observe
the visitors one receives, since not everyone who comes calling
can be trusted.

leonidas: King of Sparta (540 – 480 BC); commander of the
7,000 allied Greek forces charged with the responsibility of
stopping the advance of the 25,000-strong Persian army at
the narrow mountain pass of Thermophylae in 480 BC.

luandino: pseudonym of Jose Vieira Mateus da Graca (4 May
1935 –); award-winning Portuguese-born writer of fiction,
essayist and musicologist whose works, drawing upon his
experience of life among the black population in the
musseques (slums) of Luanda, portray the harsh realities
of Portuguese colonial rule in Africa. Devoted to the struggle
for independence, he was sentenced to fourteen years in
various prisons, eight of them in the notorious Tarrafal
concentration camp in Cape Verde.

mamman vatsa: Maj-Gen Mamman Jiya Vatsa (3 December
1940 – 5 March 1986); a soldier, poet, writer of short stories
for children and Minister of Federal Capital Territory,
executed by the Gen. Ibrahim Babangida administration in
which he served for his alleged role in a phantom coup plot.

marcello: Carlos Marcello (6 February 1910 – 3 March 1993);
godfather of the Mafia in New Orleans.

margaret: Margaret Hilda Thatcher (13 October 1925 –);
British Conservative Party politician and first female prime
minister (1979 – 1990).

mary: Mary Allin Travers (9 November 1936 – 16 September 2009); an American singer and songwriter; clarion-voiced third of the folk pop group Peter, Paul and Mary, one of the most successful folk-singing groups of the 1960s. Their hit songs, "Blowin' in the Wind", "If I Had a Hammer" and "Where Are All the Flowers Gone", became anthems of the protest movements of the 1960s.
Allusions are to The Hammer Song, "If I Had a Hammer", and "This Land is Your Land" by Woody Guthrie.

mboya: Tom (Thomas Joseph Odhiambo) Mboya (15 August 1930 – 5 July 1969); prominent Kenyan politician during Jomo Kenyatta's government; founder of the Nairobi People's Congress Party and key figure in the formation of the Kenya African National Union (KANU), gunned down on 5 July 1969 on Moi Avenue by a Kikuyu tribesman.

mehta: Tyeb Mehta (25 July 1925 – 2 July 2009); one of India's most celebrated Modernist painters whose paintings raised numerous questions on the human condition.
The allusion in the poem is to his 1997 landmark painting, *Mahishasura*.

menchu: Vicente Menchu; Quiche Indian community leader, founder of the Community of Peasant Unity or CUC and father of the winner of the 1992 Nobel Peace Prize and human rights activist, Rigoberta Menchu, killed when the Spanish embassy in Guatemala City was set ablaze on 31 December 1980, on the orders of Gen Romeo Lucas Garcia, to take out thirty-nine campesinos, who had occupied the ambassador's office to protest the atrocities of the Guatemalan army in El Quiche province.

mulungu: the Supreme Creator God of the Nyamwezi people of Tanzania; a sky god who occasionally rumbles like thunder; a thunder god.

nkwobi (Igbo): a delicacy made of soft, well-cooked cowleg seasoned with finely ground crayfish, fresh pepper, Maggi or any other flavouring and a thick sauce of potash and palm oil. It is served in a small mortar, garnished with slices of onions and chopped *utazi* leaves. Nkwobi is served as an accompaniment to an *ugba* dish and taken with palmwine or Stout.

not every han carry cutlass kin kill
yet you get for watch cutlass an han'
(although it isn't every hand that wields a cutlass that can kill
still you've got to watch both cutlass and hand)

A Creole proverb, it calls for circumspection in all human relationships.

orange yellow fine for eye
how you know e sweet
(how can you tell the sweetness of an orange
from its seemingly attractive colour)

A Creole proverb warning against hasty decision or judgment based on appearance.

phalaris: a cruel and despotic ruler of Agrigento in southern Sicily (approx. 570 – 554 BC), who is alleged to have engaged in cannibalism. He is said to have built a bronze bull in which his victims were roasted alive. Killed in a revolt, he was burned in his brazen bull.

philip: Philip II (382 BC), king of Macedonia (360 – 336 BC) and father of Alexander the Great; forger of the first Western national army; reformer and skilled diplomat, who took advantage of the divisions and quarrels between the Greek city states to defeat and bring them under Macedonian rule, so that by 339 BC all of Greece was under his control.

rizal: Dr Jose Rizal (19 December 1861 – 30 December 1896); premier Filipino national hero, ophthalmic surgeon, sculptor, artist, poet, novelist and dramatist whose revolutionary works such as *Noli Mo Tangere* (*Touch Me Not*) and *El Filibusterismo* (*The Subversive*), which expose the injustices committed by Spanish civil and clerical officials, and his articles in *La Solidaridad*, advocating political, religious and social reforms, helped inspire the Philippine Revolution of 1896 – 1898 that ended two hundred years of Spanish colonial rule.

serena: favourite niece of Emperor Theodosius I (11 January 347 – 17 January 395 AD), who in 384 arranged her marriage to Stilicho to secure the loyalty of this promising military officer.

son my (Vietnamese): the **Son My** or **My Lai Massacre**; village in South Vietnam where a platoon of United States soldiers brutally murdered over 400 women, children and elderly people on 16 March 1968.

sosa: Mercedes Sosa (9 July 1935 – 4 October 2009); award-winning, internationally acclaimed Argentine singer and activist.

srebrenica: the **Srebrenica Massacre**; a town in Bosnia Herzegovenia where more than 8,000 Bosnian Muslims, mainly men and boys, were massacred by units of the Army of Republika Srpska under the command of Gen. Ratko Mladic in July 1995.

stilicho: Flavius Stilicho (359 – 22 August 408 AD); a high-ranking Roman general and statesman of the Western Roman Empire.
Born in what is present-day Germany of a Vandal father, who had served as commander of barbarian auxillaries in the army of Emperor Valens (364 – 378 AD), and a Roman

mother, he entered the imperial army at an early age as a cavalry officer, rapidly rising through the ranks to become *magister militum* (Master of the Soldiery) in 385 following his defeat of the rebel and pretender, Eugenius. In appreciation of his loyal service to the empire, the Emperor Theodosius I married his niece, Serena, to Stilicho, thus forming a blood tie with him and ensuring that his loyalty would always be with his family.

talib: Lt. Col. Talib Ayombekov; a Tajik civil war-era warlord; an officer of the border police and renegade commander of the remote Southeastern Province of Gorno Badakashan; one of the region's main drug lords who also runs a cigarette- and gun-smuggling business.

tambo: Oliver Reginald Tambo (27 October 1917 – 24 April 1993); founding member and first Secretary General of the African National Congress (ANC) Youth League and later President of the ANC.

taras: Taras Hryhorovych Shevchenko (9 March 1814 – 10 March 1861); Ukrainian poet, artist and painter, whose writings formed the foundation of modern Ukrainian Literature. His poetry immensely contributed to the growth of Ukrainian national consciousness.

themistocles: (Greek) lit. "Glory of the Law"; Athenian populist politician and general of superlative skill and foresight, he rose to prominence in the early years of Athenian democracy. Elected archon in 493 BC, he took steps to advance the naval power of Athens and distinguished himself as the saviour of all Greece. During the first Persian invasion of Greece, Themistocles was one of the ten Athenian generals who fought at the Battle of Marathon and the de facto *commander of the Allied Greek Fleet at Artemisium and architect of the defeat of the Persians at the Battle of Salamis during the second Persian invasion of Greece in 480 BC.*

tuol sleng: (Khmer) lit." Hill of the Poisonous Trees"; the notorious **Security Prison 21 (S – 21)**; a former high school in Phnom Penh converted by the Khmer Rouge in May 1976 into a prison where an estimated 20,000 people were systematically imprisoned, interrogated, tortured and murdered.

whydah: the flagship of the pirate, Black Sam Bellamy, which sank in a storm off Cape Cod on 26 April 1717 with about five tons of silver, gold, gold dust and jewellery.

xibalba be: lit. "Place of fear" or "Place of phantoms"; in Maya mythology, a dangerous underworld ruled by the demons Vucub Caquix and Han Came; the place of death ruled by twelve gods or powerful rulers known as the Lords of Xibalba.

Kraftgriots

Also in the series (POETRY) *continued*

Joe Ushie: *A Reign of Locusts* (2004)
Paulina Mabayoje: *The Colours of Sunset* (2004)
Segun Adekoya: *Guinea Bites and Sahel Blues* (2004)
Ebi Yeibo: *Maiden Lines* (2004)
Barine Ngaage: *Rhythms of Crisis* (2004)
Funso Aiyejina: *I,The Supreme & Other Poems* (2004)
'Lere Oladitan: *Boolekaja: Lagos Poems 1* (2005)
Seyi Adigun: *Bard on the Shore* (2005)
Famous Dakolo: *A Letter to Flora* (2005)
Olawale Durojaiye: *An African Night* (2005)
G. 'Ebinyo Ogbowei: *let the honey run & other poems* (2005)
Joe Ushie: *Popular Stand & Other Poems* (2005)
Gbemisola Adeoti: *Naked Soles* (2005)
Aj. Dagga Tolar: *This Country is not a Poem* (2005)
Tunde Adeniran: *Labyrinthine Ways* (2006)
Sophia Obi: *Tears in a Basket* (2006)
Tonyo Biriabebe: *Undercurrents* (2006)
Ademola O. Dasylva: *Songs of Odamolugbe* (2006), winner, 2006 ANA/Cadbury
    poetry prize
George Ehusani: *Flames of Truth* (2006)
Abubakar Gimba: *This Land of Ours* (2006)
G. 'Ebinyo Ogbowei: *the heedless ballot box* (2006)
Hyginus Ekwuazi: *Love Apart* (2006), winner, 2007 ANA/NDDC Gabriel Okara
    poetry prize and winner, 2007 ANA/Cadbury poetry prize
Abubakar Gimba: *Inner Rumblings* (2006)
Albert Otto: *Letters from the Earth* (2007)
Aj. Dagga Tolar: *Darkwaters Drunkard* (2007)
Idris Okpanachi: *The Eaters of the Living* (2007), winner, 2008 ANA/Cadbury
    poetry prize
Tubal-Cain: *Mystery in Our Stream* (2007), winner, 2006 ANA/NDDC Gabriel
    Okara poetry prize
John Iwuh: *Ashes & Daydreams* (2007)
Sola Owonibi: *Chants to the Ancestors* (2007)
Doutimi Kpakiama: *Salute to our Mangrove Giants* (2008)
Halima M. Usman: *Spellbound* (2008)
Hyginus Ekwuazi: *Dawn Into Moonlight: All Around Me Dawning* (2008), winner,
    2008 ANA/NDDC Gabriel Okara poetry prize
Ismail Bala Garba & Abdullahi Ismaila (eds.): *Pyramids: An Anthology of Poems
    from Northern Nigeria* (2008)
Denja Abdullahi: *Abuja Nunyi (This is Abuja)* (2008)
Japhet Adeneye: *Poems for Teenagers* (2008)
Seyi Hodonu: *A Tale of Two in Time (Letters to Susan)* (2008)
Ibukun Babarinde: *Running Splash of Rust and Gold* (2008)
Chris Ngozi Nkoro: *Trails of a Distance* (2008)

111

(POETRY) continued

Tunde Adeniran: *Beyond Finalities* (2008)
Abba Abdulkareem: *A Bard's Balderdash* (2008)
Ifeanyi D. Ogbonnaya: ... *And Pigs Shall Become House Cleaners* (2008)
Ebinyo Ogbowei: *the town crier's song* (2009)
Ebinyo Ogbowei: *song of a dying river* (2009)
Sophia Obi-Apoko: *Floating Snags* (2009)
Akachi Adimora-Ezeigbo: *Heart Songs* (2009), winner, 2009 ANA/Cadbury poetry prize
Hyginus Ekwuazi: *The Monkey's Eyes* (2009)
Seyi Adigun: *Prayer for the Mwalimu* (2009)
Faith A. Brown: *Endless Season* (2009)
B.M. Dzukogi: *Midnight Lamp* (2009)
B.M. Dzukogi: *These Last Tears* (2009)
Chimezie Ezechukwu: *The Nightingale* (2009)
Ummi Kaltume Abdullahi: *Tiny Fingers* (2009)
Ismaila Bala & Ahmed Maiwada (eds.): *Fireflies: An Anthology of New Nigerian Poetry* (2009)
Eugenia Abu: *Don't Look at Me Like That* (2009)
Data Osa Don-Pedro: *You Are Gold and Other Poems* (2009)
Sam Omatseye: *Mandela's Bones and Other Poems* (2009)
Sam Omatseye: *Dear Baby Ramatu* (2009)
C.O. Iyimoga: *Fragments in the Air* (2010)
Bose Ayeni-Tsevende: *Streams* (2010)
Seyi Hodonu: *Songs from My Mother's Heart* (2010), winner ANA/NDDC Gabriel Okara poetry prize, 2010
Akachi Adimora-Ezeigbo: *Waiting for Dawn* (2010)
Hyginus Ekwuazi: *That Other Country* (2010), winner, ANA/Cadbury poetry prize, 2010
Tosin Otitoju: *Comrade* (2010)
Arnold Udoka: *Poems Across Borders* (2010)
Arnold Udoka: *The Gods Are So Silent & Other Poems* (2010)
Abubakar Othman: *The Passions of Cupid* (2010)
Okinba Launko: *Dream-Seeker on Divining Chain* (2010)
'kufre ekanem: *the ant eaters* (2010)
McNezer Fasehun: *Ever Had a Dear Sister* (2010)
Baba S. Umar: *A Portrait of My People* (2010)
Gimba Kakanda: *Safari Pants* (2010)
Sam Omatseye: *Lion Wind & Other Poems* (2011)
Ify Omalicha: *Now that Dreams are Born* (2011)
Karo Okokoh: *Souls of a Troubadour* (2011)
Ada Onyebuenyi, Chris Ngozi Nkoro, Ebere Chukwu (eds): *Uto Nka: An Anthology of Literature for Fresh Voices* (2011)
Mabel Osakwe: *Desert Songs of Bloom* (2011)
Pious Okoro: *Vultures of Fortune & Other Poems* (2011)
Godwin Yina: *Clouds of Sorrows* (2011)
Nnimmo Bassey: *I Will Not Dance to Your Beat* (2011)

Denja Abdullahi: *A Thousand Years of Thirst* (2011)
Enoch Ojotisa: *Commoner's Speech* (2011)
Rowland Timi Kpakiama: *Bees and Beetles* (2011)
Niyi Osundare: *Random Blues* (2011)
Lawrence Ogbo Ugwuanyi: *Let Them Not Run* (2011)
Saddiq M. Dzukogi: *Canvas* (2011)
Arnold Udoka: *Running with My Rivers* (2011)
Olusanya Bamidele: *Erased Without a Trace* (2011)
Olufolake Jegede: *Treasure Pods* (2012)
Karo Okokoh: *Songs of a Griot* (2012), winner. ANA/NDDC Gabriel Okara
   poetry prize, 2012
Musa Idris Okpanachi: *From the Margins of Paradise* (2012)
John Martins Agba: *The Fiend and Other Poems* (2012)
Sunnie Ododo: *Broken Pitchers* (2012)
'Kunmi Adeoti: *Epileptic City* (2012)
Ibiwari Ikiriko: *Oily Tears of the Delta* (2012)
Bala Dalhatu: *Moonlights* (2012)
Karo Okokoh: *Manna for the Mind* (2012)
Chika O. Agbo: *The Fury of the Gods* (2012)
Emmanuel C. S. Ojukwu: *Beneath the Sagging Roof* (2012)
Amirikpa Oyigbenu: *Cascades and Flakes* (2012)
Ebi Yeibo: *Shadows of the Setting Sun* (2012)
Chikaoha Agoha: *Shreds of Thunder* (2012)
Mark Okorie: *Terror Verses* (2012)
Clemmy Igwebike-Ossi: *Daisies in the Desert* (2012)
Idris Amali: *Back Again (At the Foothills of Greed)* (2012)
Akachi Adimora-Ezeigbo: *Dancing Masks* (2013)